AF413558

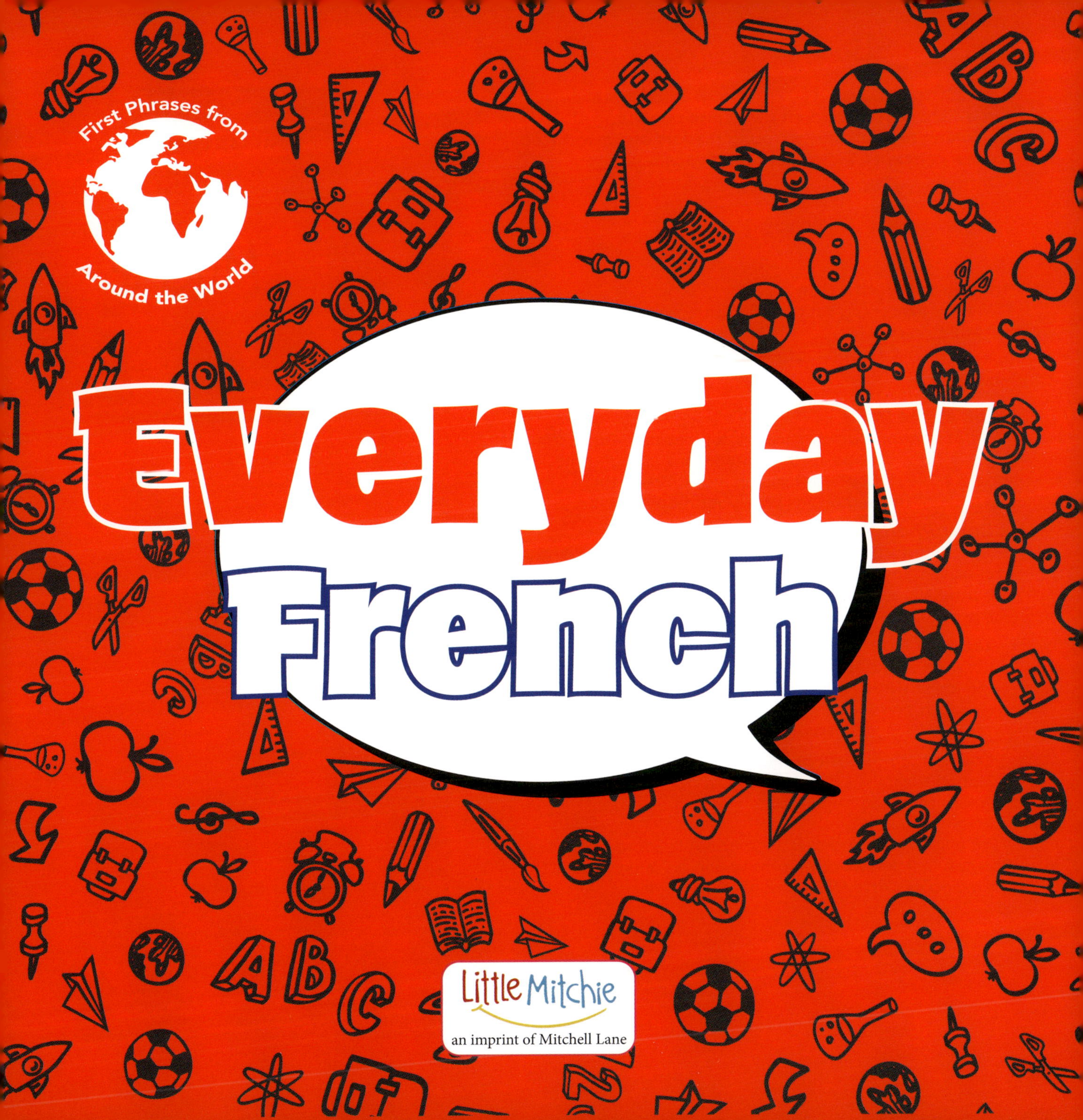

First Phrases from Around the World
Everyday French
Little Mitchie
an imprint of Mitchell Lane

Creating Young Nonfiction Readers

Little Mitchie lets children delve into nonfiction at beginning reading levels. Young readers are introduced to new concepts, facts, ideas, and vocabulary.

Tips for Reading Nonfiction with Young Readers

Talk about Nonfiction

Begin by explaining that nonfiction books give us information that is true. The book will be organized around a specific topic or idea, and we may learn new facts through reading.

Look at the Parts

Most nonfiction books have helpful features. Our *Little Mitchie* titles include color photographs and graphic aids, a table of contents, and an index. Share the purpose of these features with your reader.

Color Photos and Graphic Aids

A lot of information can be found by "reading" photos, charts, maps, and other graphic aids found within nonfiction texts. Help your reader learn more about the different ways information can be displayed.

Table of Contents

Located at the front of the book, this list shows the big ideas within the text and the page numbers where they can be found.

Index

Located at the back of the book, an index is an alphabetical list of topics and the page numbers where they can be found.

With a little help and guidance about reading nonfiction, you can feel good about introducing a young reader to the world of *Little Mitchie* nonfiction books.

Mitchell Lane
PUBLISHERS

2001 SW 31st Avenue
Hallandale, FL 33009
www.mitchelllanepub.com

First Edition, 2026.

Author: Kim Thompson
Designer: Kathy Walsh
Editor: Tricia Hoffman

Names/credits: Kim Thompson
Title: First Phrases from Around the World
 Everyday French
Description: Hallandale, FL:
Mitchell Lane Publishers, [2026]

Series: First Phrases from Around the World
Library bound ISBN: 979-8-89260-540-3
Paperback ISBN: 979-8-89260-582-3
eBook ISBN: 979-8-89260-548-9

Little Mitchie is an imprint of
Mitchell Lane Publishers

PHOTO CREDITS
Cover and Title pg: Adobe Stock: iukhym_vova, smile3377; Doodle Art Adobe: devitaayu, FourLeafLover, wanchana, veekicl, Rizky, mhatzapa, Kebon doodle, Asyam Design, piixypeach, syoko; p16, bobex73, jovo; p17, deagreez; p 18, Konstantin Postumitenko, LIGHTFIELD STUDIOS; p19, MandicJovan, Tamara Sales: istock: background, rica nohara; p5, riza1999; p13, Bet_Noire: Shutterstock: p4, Yulia Prizova, Valua Vitaly, Antonio Guillem, p5, Dragana Gordic; p6, Ground Picture, Veronica Louro, Prostock-studio; p7, Sergey Novikov, Eric Isselle; p9, Master1305; p10, AI, Lucky Business Lopolo; p 11 AI; p12, Dean Drobot, Chiociolla, Chase D'animulls, Bongostock; p13, Inside Creative House; p14, Ljupco Smokovski, Ground Picture, PeopleImages.Com - Yuri A; p 15, fast-stock, Monkey Business Images; p16, Master1305; p18, Monkey Business Images;p20, Drazen Zigic, Q88, Sorapop Udomsri; p21, Lesya Dolyuk, Torychemistry, yas_creative, long island beach, DDaria Fox, Idea Route; p22, suriyachan, New Africa, Pressmaster; p23, TommyStockProject

Table of Contents

This Is Me

J'ai neuf ans.
I am nine years old.

Je m'appelle Henri.
My name is Henri.

Ceci est Moi

un
one
deux
two
trois
three
quatre
four
cinq
five
six
six
sept
seven
huit
eight
neuf
nine
dix
ten
Au revoir!
Goodbye!

People and Pets

Les gens et les animaux de compagnie

Today

Aujourd'hui c'est mercredi.

Today is Wednesday.

dimanche

Sunday

lundi

Monday

mardi

Tuesday

mercredi

Wednesday

jeudi

Thursday

vendredi

Friday

samedi

Saturday

8

Le mois est janvier.

The month is January.

janvier . . . . January

février . . . . February

mars . . . . March

avril . . . . April

mai . . . . May

juin . . . . June

juillet . . . . July

août . . . . August

septembre . . . September

octobre . . . . . . October

novembre . . . . November

décembre . . . . December

Aujourd'hui

Il fait froid dehors.
It is cold outside.

ensoleillé
sunny

chaud
hot

pluvieux
rainy

venteux
windy

9

Morning

Je me peigne les cheveux.

I comb my hair.

Je me brosse les dents.

I brush my teeth.

Matin

Je porte un pantalon bleu.

I wear blue pants.

orange	jaune	bleu	vert
orange	yellow	blue	green

violet	rouge	rose	noir	blanc
purple	red	pink	black	white

Breakfast

pain grillé
toast

du jus d'orange
orange juice

lard
bacon

œuf
egg

Petit-déjeuner

autobus scolaire
school bus

carnet de notes
notebook

sac à dos
backpack

School

J'ai lu.

I read.

Je fais des maths.

I do math.

École

professeure
teacher

bureau
desk

Time to Play

Veux-tu jouer avec moi?
Will you play with me?
Oui!
Yes!

Je cours.
I run.

Je swingue.
I swing.

Il est temps de jouer

Neighborhood

Je fais signe à mon ami.
I wave to my friend.

Je vais au magasin.
I go to the store.

Quartier

Combien cela coûte-t-il?

How much does this cost?

Dinner

Oui s'il vous plait.
Yes, please.

Non merci.
No, thank you.

Excusez-moi.
Excuse me.

Dîner

croissant
croissant

baguette
baguette

quiche
quiche

frits
fries

pizza
pizza

Night

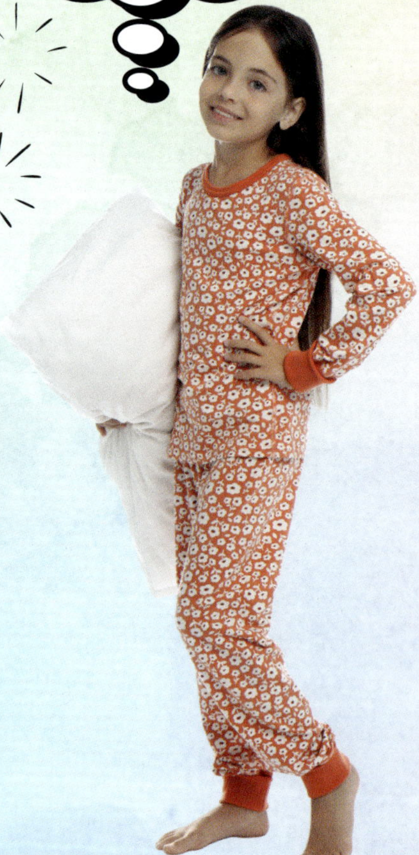

Je vais me coucher.
I go to bed.

Je ferme les yeux.
I close my eyes.

Nuit

23

Index

About French

French is the first language of approximately 220 million people. Many others speak it as a second language. It is the fifth most common language in the world. The top five countries where French is spoken are France, the Democratic Republic of the Congo, Algeria, Morocco, and Germany. About 20 African nations declare French as an official language. French is also the official language in the Caribbean country of Haiti. One in five Canadians speak French as their first language. Most French-speakers in Canada live in the province of Québec.